TEAS EXAM ESSENTIALS

Chioma Okeke

Table Of Contents

Chapter 1: Introduction to the TEAS Exam — 3
    What is the TEAS Exam? — 3
    Why is the TEAS Exam Important for Nursing School Admission? — 4
    How to Register for the TEAS Exam — 5
    Understanding the TEAS Exam Format and Content — 7

Chapter 2: Reading Comprehension Practice Questions — 9
    Strategies for Improving Reading Comprehension Skills — 9
    Sample Reading Comprehension Questions
        Answer Key and Explanations for Reading Comprehension Practice Questions

Chapter 3: Mathematics Practice Questions — 11
    Essential Math Skills for the TEAS Exam — 11
    Sample Mathematics Questions — 13
        Answer Key and Explanations for Mathematics Practice Questions

Chapter 4: Science Practice Questions — 15
    Review of Key Science Concepts for the TEAS Exam — 15
    Sample Science Questions — 16
    Answer Key and Explanations for Science Practice Questions

Chapter 5: English and Language Usage Practice Questions — 19
    Grammar and Vocabulary Skills for the TEAS Exam — 19
    Sample English and Language Usage Questions — 20
    Answer Key and Explanations for English and Language Usage Practice Questions — 22

Chapter 6: Online Practice Quizzes — 24

    Utilizing Online Resources for TEAS Exam Preparation — 24

    Online Practice Quizzes for Reading Comprehension — 25

    Online Practice Quizzes for Mathematics — 26

    Online Practice Quizzes for Science — 28

    Online Practice Quizzes for English and Language Usage — 29

Chapter 7: Test-Taking Strategies and Tips — 31

    Time Management Techniques for the TEAS Exam — 31

    Approaches to Eliminating Answer Choices — 32

    Effective Guessing Strategies — 33

    Tips for Managing Test Anxiety — 35

Chapter 8: Conclusion and Next Steps — 38

    Assessing Your TEAS Exam Performance — 38

    Developing a Study Schedule for Continued Preparation — 39

    Additional Resources for TEAS Exam Review — 41

Appendix: TEAS Exam Resources and References — 43

Chapter 1: Introduction to the TEAS Exam

What is the TEAS Exam?

If you are considering a career in nursing and have set your sights on attending nursing school, then you have likely come across the TEAS exam. The Test of Essential Academic Skills (TEAS) is a standardized test that is often a requirement for admission into nursing programs across the United States.

The TEAS exam is designed to assess your academic readiness for the rigorous coursework that awaits you in nursing school. It evaluates your knowledge and understanding in four main subject areas: Reading, Mathematics, Science, and English and Language Usage. Each section is timed, with a total test time of around four hours. The test is multiple-choice, with a total of 170 questions.

The Reading section of the TEAS exam measures your ability to understand and analyze written passages. It assesses your comprehension skills, as well as your ability to draw conclusions, make inferences, and identify main ideas.

The Mathematics section covers a wide range of topics, including basic arithmetic, algebra, and measurement. It evaluates your ability to solve mathematical problems and apply mathematical concepts to real-world scenarios.

The Science section tests your knowledge in areas such as anatomy and physiology, biology, chemistry, and the scientific method. It assesses your understanding of scientific concepts and your ability to apply them to various situations.

The English and Language Usage section focuses on your grammar, punctuation, and vocabulary skills. It evaluates your ability to identify and correct grammatical errors, as well as your understanding of word usage and sentence structure.

Preparing for the TEAS exam is crucial to your success. There are many resources available to help you study and practice, including TEAS exam practice tests and quizzes. These practice materials can give you a sense of the types of questions you will encounter on the actual exam and help you identify areas where you may need additional review.

By dedicating time and effort to studying for the TEAS exam, you can increase your chances of achieving a high score and gaining admission into the nursing program of your choice. Remember, the TEAS exam is just one piece of the admissions puzzle, so be sure to also focus on maintaining a strong academic record, gathering letters of recommendation, and writing a compelling personal statement.

In conclusion, the TEAS exam is a vital step in your journey towards becoming a nurse. It evaluates your academic readiness and ensures that you have the necessary knowledge and skills to succeed in nursing school. By familiarizing yourself with the exam format and practicing with TEAS exam practice tests and quizzes, you can approach the test with confidence and increase your chances of admission into nursing school.

Why is the TEAS Exam Important for Nursing School Admission?

The TEAS Exam, also known as the Test of Essential Academic Skills, is a critical component of the nursing school admission process. Aspiring nurses must understand the significance of this exam and adequately prepare for it in order to increase their chances of gaining admission to their desired nursing program.

One of the primary reasons why the TEAS Exam is essential for nursing school admission is that it assesses the fundamental academic skills necessary for success in nursing education. These skills include reading comprehension, mathematics, science, and English language usage. Nursing school curricula are rigorous and demanding, and students need a solid foundation in these areas to excel in their coursework.

Additionally, the TEAS Exam evaluates critical thinking and problem-solving abilities, which are vital skills for nurses. In the healthcare field, nurses often encounter complex situations that require quick thinking and effective decision-making. By assessing these skills, the TEAS Exam ensures that prospective nursing students have the aptitude to handle the challenges they will face during their nursing education and future careers.

Furthermore, nursing schools utilize the TEAS Exam as a tool to select the most qualified applicants for their programs. With limited spots available in nursing programs, schools need a reliable method to identify individuals who have the potential to succeed in their programs. The TEAS Exam provides an objective measure of applicants' academic abilities and helps schools make informed decisions during the admission process.

For individuals aspiring to attend nursing school, dedicating time and effort to prepare for the TEAS Exam is crucial. By familiarizing themselves with the exam format, content, and question types, aspiring nurses can boost their confidence and performance on the day of the exam. Practice tests and quizzes specifically designed for the TEAS Exam are valuable resources for improving test-taking skills, identifying areas that require additional study, and gaining familiarity with the exam's time constraints.

In conclusion, the TEAS Exam is of utmost importance for individuals who want to attend nursing school. It evaluates essential academic skills, critical thinking abilities, and serves as a criterion for nursing program admission. By recognizing the significance of the TEAS Exam and dedicating time to prepare for it, aspiring nurses can enhance their chances of gaining admission to nursing school and embarking on a fulfilling career in the healthcare field.

How to Register for the TEAS Exam

Registering for the TEAS (Test of Essential Academic Skills) exam is an important step for anyone who wants to pursue a career in nursing. The TEAS exam is a standardized test that assesses the academic preparedness of individuals seeking admission to nursing programs. To ensure a smooth and successful registration process, it is essential to follow these steps:

1. Research Available Testing Centers: The first step in registering for the TEAS exam is to find a testing center near you. The TEAS exam is administered by the Assessment Technologies Institute (ATI), and they have authorized testing centers across the United States. Visit the ATI website or contact their customer service to find the nearest testing center.

2. Determine the Registration Process: Each testing center may have slightly different registration procedures, so it is crucial to contact your chosen testing center to understand their specific requirements. Inquire about registration fees, necessary identification documents, and any deadlines you need to be aware of.

3. Create an ATI Account: Before registering for the TEAS exam, you will need to create an account on the ATI website. Visit their website, click on the "Create an Account" button, and provide the required information. This account will be used not only for registration but also for accessing your TEAS scores and other related information.

4. Select a Test Date: Once you have created an ATI account, you can select a test date. It is important to choose a date that gives you enough time to prepare. Consider your study schedule and other commitments while selecting the test date.

5. Pay the Registration Fee: To complete the registration process, you will need to pay the required registration fee. The fee covers the cost of administering the TEAS exam, and it may vary depending on the testing center. Make sure to check the payment options accepted by the testing center and complete the payment within the specified deadline.

6. Review the TEAS Exam Policies: Before taking the TEAS exam, it is crucial to familiarize yourself with the exam policies. These policies may include rules regarding personal belongings, calculators, breaks, and identification requirements. Knowing and adhering to these policies will ensure a smooth testing experience.

By following these steps, you can successfully register for the TEAS exam and take a step closer to your dream of attending nursing school. Remember to stay organized, plan ahead, and use available resources, such as TEAS exam practice tests and quizzes, to prepare effectively for the exam. Good luck on your journey to becoming a nurse!

Understanding the TEAS Exam Format and Content

The TEAS (Test of Essential Academic Skills) is a crucial exam for individuals aspiring to pursue a career in nursing. This subchapter aims to provide a comprehensive understanding of the TEAS exam format and content, helping individuals effectively prepare for this important assessment.

The TEAS exam consists of four sections: Reading, Mathematics, Science, and English and Language Usage. Each section is designed to evaluate the test-taker's knowledge and proficiency in specific academic areas relevant to nursing education.

The Reading section assesses the individual's ability to comprehend written passages and draw logical conclusions. It includes questions related to paragraph comprehension, passage comprehension, and inferences.

The Mathematics section evaluates the individual's mathematical skills, including whole numbers, fractions, decimals, percentages, ratios, proportions, and algebraic equations. It is vital for aspiring nurses to have a strong foundation in mathematics to excel in this section.

The Science section measures the individual's understanding of scientific concepts, including biology, chemistry, anatomy, physiology, and the scientific method. This section requires a solid grasp of fundamental scientific principles and their application in real-world scenarios.

The English and Language Usage section focuses on grammar, punctuation, sentence structure, and vocabulary. It assesses the individual's ability to communicate effectively in written English, a crucial skill for nurses in their professional practice.

To effectively prepare for the TEAS exam, it is important to become familiar with the format and content of each section. This can be achieved through extensive practice tests and quizzes specifically tailored to the TEAS exam. By practicing with authentic questions similar to those found in the actual exam, individuals can gain confidence and enhance their performance.

Numerous resources are available to assist individuals in their TEAS exam preparation. Online platforms, study guides, and review books provide detailed explanations, strategies, and practice questions that mirror the content and difficulty level of the exam.

In conclusion, understanding the TEAS exam format and content is essential for individuals aspiring to attend nursing school. By familiarizing themselves with the sections and content of the exam and engaging in rigorous practice tests and quizzes, individuals can increase their chances of achieving a high score and pursuing their dream of becoming a nurse.

Chapter 2: Reading Comprehension Practice Questions

Strategies for Improving Reading Comprehension Skills

Reading comprehension is a crucial skill for aspiring nurses, as it forms the basis of effective communication and critical thinking in the healthcare profession. Developing strong reading comprehension skills can help you excel in your nursing education and perform well on the TEAS exam. In this subchapter, we will explore effective strategies for improving your reading comprehension abilities.

1. Preview the Text: Before diving into a passage, take a few moments to preview it. Skim through the headings, subheadings, and any bold or italicized text. This will give you a general idea of the content and help you generate questions or predictions about the material.

2. Active Reading: Engage with the text actively by underlining or highlighting key points, circling unfamiliar terms, and jotting down notes or questions in the margins. This will keep you focused and help you retain information. Additionally, try summarizing each paragraph in a few words to ensure you understand the main ideas.

3. Build Vocabulary: Nursing is a field rich in specialized terminology. Enhancing your vocabulary will not only improve your reading comprehension but also aid in understanding medical jargon later on. Make it a habit to look up and learn new words, especially those commonly found in nursing textbooks and articles.

4. Practice Time Management: Time management is essential for success in the TEAS exam. Allocate a specific amount of time for each passage during practice tests to simulate real exam conditions. Be mindful of the clock and aim to complete each passage within the allotted time frame.

5. Practice Active Reading Strategies: Employ various active reading strategies like asking questions, making connections to prior knowledge, and visualizing concepts. This will enhance your understanding and engagement with the material.

6. Take Practice Tests: Regularly take practice tests and quizzes specifically designed for the TEAS exam. These assessments will help you gauge your progress, identify areas of weakness, and familiarize yourself with the format and content of the exam.

7. Seek Additional Resources: Utilize additional resources such as study guides, online tutorials, and flashcards to reinforce your reading comprehension skills. These resources can provide valuable tips, strategies, and practice exercises to further improve your abilities.

By implementing these strategies, you can enhance your reading comprehension skills, ensuring success on the TEAS exam and setting a strong foundation for your nursing education. Remember to practice regularly, seek support when needed, and approach each passage with a curious and engaged mindset.

Chapter 3: Mathematics Practice Questions

Essential Math Skills for the TEAS Exam

Mathematics is a fundamental subject that plays a crucial role in the nursing profession. To succeed in the Test of Essential Academic Skills (TEAS) exam and pursue a career in nursing, it is essential to have a strong foundation in math. In this subchapter, we will explore the key math skills you need to master for the TEAS exam.

1. Arithmetic: Arithmetic forms the basis of math skills required for nursing. It includes operations like addition, subtraction, multiplication, and division. You should be comfortable performing calculations with whole numbers, fractions, decimals, and percentages. These skills are vital for medication dosage calculations and understanding medical charts.

2. Algebra: Algebraic skills are necessary for solving equations and understanding patterns. You should be able to solve linear equations, work with variables, and interpret graphs. These concepts are essential for understanding dosage calculations, drug administration, and analyzing patient data.

3. Geometry: Geometry skills come into play when dealing with measurements, shapes, and spatial relationships. You should be familiar with concepts like area, perimeter, volume, and angles. These skills are necessary for interpreting diagrams, understanding medical imaging, and measuring patient conditions accurately.

4. Statistics and Probability: Nursing professionals often encounter statistical data and probability concepts. You should be comfortable interpreting graphs, calculating averages, and understanding basic statistical measures. Additionally, understanding probability helps in making informed decisions based on the likelihood of certain outcomes.

5. Data Analysis: Data analysis skills involve organizing and interpreting numerical data. You should be able to identify trends, draw conclusions, and make predictions based on the given information. These skills are essential for evidence-based practice and understanding research findings.

To solidify your math skills, it is crucial to practice regularly using TEAS exam practice tests and quizzes. These resources will help you become familiar with the types of math problems you may encounter on the exam, allowing you to identify areas where you need improvement.

Remember, mastering math skills for the TEAS exam is not just about passing the test; it is about developing a foundation that will serve you throughout your nursing career. A strong math background will enable you to provide accurate medication dosages, interpret patient data effectively, and make informed decisions in critical situations.

By dedicating time and effort to mastering essential math skills, you will be better prepared for the TEAS exam and well-equipped to succeed in nursing school.

Mathematics Questions

In order to succeed in nursing school, it is essential to have a solid foundation in mathematics. The TEAS (Test of Essential Academic Skills) exam is a crucial step towards entering nursing school, and it includes a Mathematics section that evaluates your command of mathematical concepts and problem-solving skills.

1. Fractions and Decimals: One of the fundamental concepts in mathematics is working with fractions and decimals. Practice questions in this section will test your ability to add, subtract, multiply, and divide fractions and decimals. You will also encounter questions that require you to convert fractions to decimals and vice versa.

2. Ratios and Proportions: Understanding ratios and proportions is essential for nurses, as they often need to calculate medication dosages. Sample questions in this category will assess your ability to solve problems involving ratios, proportions, and percentages. You will be asked to solve problems related to dosage calculations and determine appropriate medication administration.

3. Algebraic Equations: Algebra is another critical area of mathematics for aspiring nurses. Questions in this section will assess your skills in solving linear equations, working with inequalities, and simplifying algebraic expressions. You may also encounter word problems that require you to set up and solve equations.

4. Data Interpretation and Analysis: As a nurse, you will frequently encounter data and statistics. This section will test your ability to interpret and analyze graphs, tables, and charts. You will be asked to calculate averages, percentages, and probabilities based on given data.

5. Geometry and Measurement: Understanding basic geometric principles and measurements is necessary for nurses in various situations, such as wound care and medication calculations. Sample questions in this area will assess your knowledge of geometric shapes, measurements, and conversions between different units of measurement.

By learning these strategies, you will not only enhance your problem-solving abilities but also gain confidence in tackling the mathematics section of the TEAS exam. With diligent practice and a solid grasp of these mathematical concepts, you will be well-prepared to excel in the TEAS exam and thrive in nursing school.

Chapter 4: Science Practice Questions

Review of Key Science Concepts for the TEAS Exam

Aspiring nurses who want to attend nursing school understand the importance of the TEAS exam. This subchapter titled "Review of Key Science Concepts for the TEAS Exam" aims to provide an understanding of the essential science concepts necessary to excel in the TEAS exam. By reviewing these concepts, students can enhance their knowledge and boost their confidence for success in the exam.

The TEAS exam evaluates a candidate's knowledge of various scientific disciplines, including anatomy and physiology, biology, chemistry, and physics. This subchapter covers the fundamental concepts from each of these areas, ensuring a comprehensive review.

To begin, we delve into anatomy and physiology, focusing on the human body's structure and function. Key topics covered include the organization of the body, the skeletal and muscular systems, the circulatory and respiratory systems, and the digestive and reproductive systems. Understanding these concepts is crucial for answering questions related to the human body on the TEAS exam.

Moving on to biology, we explore the principles of cell biology, genetics, and evolution. Topics such as cell structure and function, DNA replication, mitosis and meiosis, inheritance patterns, and natural selection are covered. Mastery of these concepts is vital for tackling questions related to biological processes and genetics in the exam.

Next, we shift our focus to chemistry, where we review essential concepts such as atomic structure, chemical bonding, chemical reactions, and the periodic table. By understanding these concepts, students will be better equipped to answer questions on chemical properties and reactions in the TEAS exam.

Lastly, we touch upon the basics of physics, including motion, energy, and the laws of thermodynamics. Key topics explored include Newton's laws of motion, types of energy, heat transfer, and electricity. Familiarity with these concepts will enable students to tackle questions related to physics principles and their applications in healthcare.

In this subchapter, we provide practice questions to reinforce the understanding of these key science concepts. These practice exercises will help aspiring nurses gauge their knowledge and identify areas that require further attention.

By thoroughly reviewing the key science concepts covered in this subchapter, aspiring nurses can confidently approach the TEAS exam. With this knowledge, they will be well-prepared to excel in the exam and pursue their dreams of becoming nurses.

Sample Science Questions

Aspiring nurses who are preparing for the TEAS exam know that the science section can be quite challenging. To help you succeed, this subchapter presents a variety of sample science questions that will give you a taste of what to expect on the exam.

1. Biology: Which of the following organs is responsible for filtering waste products from the blood?
a) Liver
b) Kidneys
c) Pancreas
d) Gallbladder

2. Chemistry: What is the chemical symbol for sodium?
a) S
b) Na
c) So
d) N

3. Anatomy and Physiology: Which of the following is the largest bone in the human body?
a) Femur
b) Tibia
c) Humerus
d) Radius

4. Microbiology: Which of the following is NOT a type of microorganism?
a) Bacteria
b) Fungi
c) Virus
d) Mammal

5. Physics: Which of the following is an example of potential energy?
a) A rolling ball
b) A spinning top
c) A stretched rubber band
d) A moving car

6. Nutrition: Which of the following nutrients provides the highest amount of energy per gram?
a) Protein
b) Carbohydrates
c) Vitamins
d) Minerals

7. Anatomy and Physiology: What is the function of the respiratory system?
a) Pump blood throughout the body
b) Break down food into nutrients
c) Exchange oxygen and carbon dioxide
d) Remove waste products from the body

8. Chemistry: Which of the following is NOT a primary color of light?
a) Red
b) Blue
c) Yellow
d) Green

By practicing these sample science questions, you can assess your current knowledge and identify areas that require further review.

As you prepare for the TEAS exam, it is essential to practice with a variety of questions and quizzes. This book provides an extensive collection of practice tests and quizzes specifically designed for aspiring nurses. By dedicating time to studying and practicing, you will build confidence and improve your chances of achieving a successful outcome on the exam.

Stay focused and motivated, and remember that your hard work and dedication will pay off as you embark on your nursing journey. Good luck!

Chapter 5: English and Language Usage Practice Questions

Grammar and Vocabulary Skills for the TEAS Exam

In order to succeed on the TEAS exam and gain admission to nursing school, it is essential to have strong grammar and vocabulary skills. This subchapter will focus on providing you with the necessary knowledge to enhance your understanding of grammar rules and expand your vocabulary.

Effective communication is a crucial aspect of the nursing profession. Nurses must be able to accurately convey information, both verbally and in writing, to patients, doctors, and other healthcare professionals. The TEAS exam evaluates your ability to comprehend and manipulate the English language, making it essential to sharpen your grammar skills.

The subchapter will cover various topics, including parts of speech, sentence structure, verb tenses, subject-verb agreement, and punctuation.

Building a strong vocabulary is equally important, as it enables you to communicate effectively and comprehend complex medical terminology. The TEAS exam often includes passages with specialized medical vocabulary, making it crucial to expand your word bank.

To fully prepare you for the TEAS exam, this subchapter will also include a few sample practice questions specifically focused on grammar and vocabulary. These questions will simulate the actual exam format, enabling you to familiarize yourself with the types of questions you will encounter and assess your strengths and weaknesses.

By dedicating time and effort to improving your grammar and vocabulary skills, you will not only perform better on the TEAS exam but also become a more effective communicator in the nursing field. This subchapter aims to equip you with the tools and knowledge necessary to succeed, ensuring that you are well-prepared for the challenges of nursing school and your future career as a nurse.

Remember, grammar and vocabulary skills are not only valuable for the TEAS exam but also for your overall academic and professional success. Start practicing today and watch your language skills soar!

Sample English and Language Usage Questions

In order to excel in the TEAS exam and secure a place in nursing school, it is crucial to have a solid understanding of English and language usage. This subchapter aims to provide you with a set of sample questions that will help you practice and enhance your skills in this area.

1. Sentence Structure:
Which of the following sentences contains a subject, a verb, and an object?
A) The children played happily in the park.
B) Running swiftly through the field.
C) After the rain stopped.

2. Grammar:
Identify the correct form of the verb to complete the sentence.
She _____ to the doctor's office yesterday.
A) go
B) goes
C) went
D) going

3. Vocabulary:
Choose the word that is the most appropriate synonym for the given word.
Reliable:
A) Trustworthy
B) Unreliable
C) Uncertain
D) Inaccurate

4. Reading Comprehension:
Read the passage and answer the question.
Passage: The human body is composed of many intricate systems, working together to maintain optimal health. The respiratory system, for example, is responsible for the exchange of oxygen and carbon dioxide in the body.
Question: What is the main function of the respiratory system?
A) Pumping blood throughout the body
B) Digesting food
C) Controlling body temperature
D) Exchanging oxygen and carbon dioxide

5. Punctuation:
Identify the correct punctuation for the following sentence.
I am excited about the upcoming exam _____ it will be a determining factor for my acceptance into nursing school.
A) ;
B) ,
C) :
D) .

By practicing these sample questions, you will not only become familiar with the format and structure of the English and language usage section of the TEAS exam but also gain confidence in your abilities. Remember to review the correct answers and explanations for any questions you may have struggled with to further enhance your knowledge.

In addition to these sample questions, it is highly recommended to utilize practice tests and quizzes specifically designed for the TEAS exam. These resources will provide you with a comprehensive understanding of the English and language usage concepts assessed in the exam, allowing you to identify any areas that require further improvement.

By dedicating time to practicing English and language usage questions, you will be well-prepared to tackle this section of the TEAS exam, ultimately increasing your chances of success in your nursing school application. Good luck!

Answer Key and Explanations for English and Language Usage Practice Questions

As an aspiring nurse preparing for the TEAS exam, it is crucial to have a strong grasp of English and language usage skills.

Answer keys help you assess your performance and identify areas that require improvement. Each question will have a corresponding explanation that will provide you with a clear understanding of why a particular answer choice is correct or incorrect.

By reviewing the answer key and explanations, you will gain insight into the reasoning behind each correct answer. This will enable you to develop effective test-taking strategies and enhance your overall performance on the English and Language Usage section of the TEAS exam.

Our aim is to teach you how to utilize online practice questions and answers to help you understand the underlying concepts and principles.

Furthermore, the explanations will enable you to reinforce your knowledge and build confidence in your English and language usage skills. As you progress through the practice questions, you will become familiar with the types of questions commonly encountered in the TEAS exam, allowing you to better prepare yourself for the actual test.

Remember, the TEAS exam is a crucial step towards your dream of becoming a nurse. A strong foundation in English and language usage is vital for effective communication with patients, colleagues, and healthcare professionals. By dedicating time to practice and understanding the correct answers, you will be one step closer to achieving your goal of attending nursing school.

With diligent practice and a solid understanding of the concepts, you will be well-equipped to excel in this section of the TEAS exam and embark on your journey towards a rewarding nursing career.

Chapter 6: Online Practice Quizzes

Utilizing Online Resources for TEAS Exam Preparation

In today's digital age, online resources have become invaluable tools for individuals seeking to excel in various fields, including nursing. For those aspiring to attend nursing school, one of the crucial steps is preparing for the TEAS (Test of Essential Academic Skills) exam. This subchapter will explore how online resources can be effectively utilized for TEAS exam preparation, providing aspiring nurses with an edge in their quest to succeed.

The internet offers a wealth of TEAS exam practice tests and quizzes that can enhance one's understanding of the exam format, subject areas, and overall level of preparedness. These resources often mirror the actual exam, allowing individuals to familiarize themselves with the question types and time constraints they will encounter on test day. Moreover, online practice tests and quizzes enable students to identify areas where they may need additional study and focus their efforts accordingly.

One of the key advantages of online resources is their accessibility. Aspiring nurses can access TEAS exam practice tests and quizzes from anywhere, at any time, making it convenient for busy individuals to fit in study sessions around their schedules. Whether it's through websites, mobile applications, or dedicated TEAS exam preparation platforms, online resources enable students to study on the go and make the most of their available time.

Additionally, online resources often provide detailed explanations and solutions for each question, allowing students to learn from their mistakes and reinforce their understanding of the concepts being tested. This feedback loop is essential for progress and ensures that students not only know the correct answer but also comprehend the underlying principles.

Moreover, online resources foster a sense of community among aspiring nurses. Many platforms offer discussion forums, where individuals can connect with fellow test-takers, share study strategies, and seek advice from those who have successfully passed the TEAS exam. This collaborative environment can be a valuable source of support and motivation throughout the preparation process.

In conclusion, for individuals aspiring to attend nursing school, utilizing online resources for TEAS exam preparation is a wise choice. By taking advantage of the vast array of TEAS exam practice tests, quizzes, and interactive platforms available online, aspiring nurses can enhance their knowledge, sharpen their skills, and gain confidence in their ability to excel in the TEAS exam. With dedication, perseverance, and the right online resources, success in the TEAS exam is within reach, paving the way for a rewarding career in nursing.

Online Practice Quizzes for Reading Comprehension

Reading comprehension is an essential skill for aspiring nurses to master in order to excel in nursing school and succeed in their future careers.

These online practice quizzes for reading comprehension are specifically designed to simulate the format and content of the TEAS exam. They cover a wide range of topics, including passages related to healthcare, scientific research, and patient care scenarios. By regularly engaging in these quizzes, you can familiarize yourself with the types of passages you will encounter on the actual exam and improve your ability to comprehend and analyze written information.

One of the key advantages of online practice quizzes is their convenience and accessibility. You can access them from anywhere with an internet connection, allowing you to study at your own pace and on your own schedule. This flexibility is especially beneficial for individuals who may be juggling work or other commitments while preparing for the TEAS exam.

These quizzes also provide immediate feedback, allowing you to gauge your progress and identify areas for improvement. After completing a quiz, you will receive a detailed analysis of your performance, highlighting your strengths and weaknesses in reading comprehension. This feedback can guide your study plan and help you focus on areas that require additional attention.

Furthermore, online practice quizzes often come with answer explanations, providing a step-by-step breakdown of how to arrive at the correct answer. This not only helps you understand the reasoning behind the correct response but also enhances your critical thinking skills and strengthens your ability to interpret complex passages.

In addition to practice quizzes, online resources may offer timed practice tests that simulate the conditions of the actual TEAS exam. These tests can help you build stamina and improve your time management skills, ensuring that you can effectively allocate your time during the exam.

By regularly engaging in online practice quizzes and tests, you can boost your confidence, sharpen your reading comprehension skills, and maximize your chances of success on the TEAS exam. Remember to take advantage of these valuable resources as you prepare for nursing school and embark on your journey towards becoming a healthcare professional.

Online Practice Quizzes for Mathematics

Aspiring nurses understand the importance of excelling in the TEAS exam, as it serves as a crucial step towards entering nursing school. One of the key areas that students often struggle with is mathematics.

Online practice quizzes offer a comprehensive and interactive learning experience. With carefully selected questions that mirror the format and difficulty level of the actual TEAS exam, you can assess your knowledge and identify areas that require further attention. These quizzes cover various mathematical topics, including algebra, geometry, arithmetic, and data interpretation, ensuring that you have a solid foundation in the core mathematical concepts needed for success in nursing school.

Each online practice quiz is accompanied by detailed explanations for every question. This allows you to not only understand the correct answers but also grasp the underlying concepts and problem-solving techniques. By delving into these explanations, you can strengthen your understanding of mathematical principles and build the skills necessary to tackle challenging problems confidently.

Furthermore, online practice quizzes are designed to simulate the exam environment. This means that you can familiarize yourself with the time constraints and pressure associated with the TEAS exam. By practicing under similar conditions, you can enhance your time management skills and develop effective strategies to tackle the mathematics section efficiently.

Accessible anytime and anywhere, online practice quizzes offer the flexibility to fit studying into your busy schedule. Whether you have a few minutes or a couple of hours to spare, you can access the quizzes on any device with an internet connection. This convenience allows you to study at your own pace and revisit challenging topics as often as needed.

In summary, online practice quizzes for mathematics provide aspiring nurses with a valuable resource to prepare for the TEAS exam. By engaging in these quizzes, you can improve your mathematical skills, gain confidence, and enhance your chances of success in nursing school. Start practicing today and take a step closer to achieving your dream of becoming a nurse.

Online Practice Quizzes for Science

In today's digital age, preparing for exams has become more convenient and accessible than ever before. For those aspiring to attend nursing school, the TEAS exam is an essential step towards achieving their dreams. To excel in the science section of the TEAS exam, online practice quizzes can prove to be invaluable study tools.

Online practice quizzes offer a dynamic and interactive learning experience that helps individuals test their knowledge, identify weak areas, and reinforce key concepts. These quizzes are specifically designed to mirror the format and difficulty level of the actual TEAS exam, ensuring that test-takers become familiar with the types of questions they will encounter.

One of the advantages of online practice quizzes is their flexibility. With busy schedules and other commitments, aspiring nurses may find it challenging to dedicate specific time slots for studying. Online quizzes provide the convenience of accessing study materials at any time and from any location, eliminating the need for physical study materials or attending in-person classes. This flexibility allows individuals to make the most of their available time and study at their own pace.

Moreover, online practice quizzes offer immediate feedback, allowing test-takers to gauge their performance instantly. This instant feedback not only helps in identifying areas of improvement but also boosts confidence by highlighting areas of strength. By understanding their strengths and weaknesses, individuals can tailor their study plans accordingly, focusing more on topics that require additional attention.

Another significant advantage of online practice quizzes is the opportunity for repetition. Science concepts can be complex and require repeated exposure for better understanding. Online quizzes enable individuals to retake questions and quizzes multiple times, reinforcing their knowledge and enhancing retention. This repetition fosters a deeper understanding of the subject matter, ultimately leading to improved performance on the TEAS exam.

To make the most of online practice quizzes, it is important to approach them strategically. Start by taking a comprehensive diagnostic quiz to identify your baseline knowledge level. This will help you understand which areas of science you need to focus on the most. Once you have this information, create a study plan that incorporates regular practice quizzes to reinforce your learning.

In conclusion, online practice quizzes for science are an invaluable resource for those aspiring to attend nursing school and preparing for the TEAS exam. They offer flexibility, instant feedback, and the opportunity for repetition, all of which contribute to a more effective study experience. By utilizing online practice quizzes strategically, aspiring nurses can build a solid foundation in science and increase their chances of success on the TEAS exam.

Online Practice Quizzes for English and Language Usage

Online practice quizzes for English and Language Usage is a valuable resource for individuals who aspire to attend nursing school and are preparing for the TEAS exam. Aspiring nurses need to possess a strong foundation in English and language usage to excel in their profession, making this subchapter an essential tool in their exam preparation.

By utilizing the online platform, aspiring nurses can conveniently access these quizzes anytime and anywhere. This flexibility allows them to fit their study sessions seamlessly into their busy schedules, maximizing their preparation time. Moreover, the online format simulates the actual TEAS exam environment, familiarizing test-takers with the interface and enhancing their confidence during the test.

The online practice quizzes for English and Language Usage not only assess the test-takers' knowledge but also provide immediate feedback on their performance. This feedback is an invaluable tool for self-assessment, enabling individuals to identify areas of weakness and focus their study efforts accordingly. Furthermore, the quizzes offer hints and tips to guide learners through challenging questions, fostering a deeper understanding of the subject matter.

In conclusion, by utilizing the online platform, test-takers can assess their knowledge, strengthen their skills, and build confidence in their English and language usage abilities.

Chapter 7: Test-Taking Strategies and Tips

Time Management Techniques for the TEAS Exam

Aspiring nurses who are preparing to take the TEAS exam understand the importance of effective time management. The TEAS exam, or Test of Essential Academic Skills, is a crucial step in the journey towards nursing school admission. To help you make the most of your study time and perform your best on the exam, this subchapter will outline some valuable time management techniques specifically tailored for the TEAS exam.

1. Create a Study Schedule: Start by creating a study schedule that allocates specific time slots for each subject and topic. This will help you stay organized and ensure that you cover all the necessary material. Be realistic with your time allocation and factor in breaks to avoid burnout.

2. Prioritize Your Weak Areas: Identify your weak areas by taking practice tests and quizzes. Focus on these areas during your study sessions to allocate more time for improvement. By prioritizing your weaknesses, you can make targeted efforts to strengthen your knowledge and skills.

3. Utilize Practice Tests and Quizzes: Practice tests and quizzes are invaluable resources for preparing for the TEAS exam. Incorporate these into your study routine to familiarize yourself with the exam structure and refine your time management skills under exam conditions.

4. Break Down Study Material: Divide your study material into smaller, manageable sections. This will make it easier to tackle complex subjects and stay focused. By breaking down the content, you can allocate specific time slots for each section, ensuring that you cover all the material effectively.

5. Set Goals and Track Progress: Set realistic goals for each study session and track your progress. This will help you stay motivated and maintain a sense of accomplishment as you achieve your goals. Celebrate small victories along the way to keep your spirits high.

6. Practice Time-Management Techniques: During your practice tests and quizzes, practice time-management techniques such as skimming passages, quickly identifying key information, and efficiently answering questions. These techniques will help you save time during the actual exam and improve your overall score.

By implementing these time management techniques as part of your TEAS exam preparation, you can optimize your study time, improve your knowledge and skills, and increase your chances of success. Remember, effective time management is not only about studying harder but also about studying smarter. Good luck on your TEAS exam journey!

Approaches to Eliminating Answer Choices

One of the most effective strategies for success on the TEAS exam is to learn how to eliminate answer choices. Aspiring nurses who are preparing for the exam understand the importance of mastering this skill, as it can greatly improve their chances of selecting the correct answer.

Eliminating answer choices involves carefully analyzing each option and systematically ruling out those that are clearly incorrect. This approach is particularly helpful when you are unsure of the correct answer or when you are faced with confusing or complex questions. By eliminating obviously incorrect choices, you increase your chances of selecting the right answer even if you are not entirely sure.

To effectively eliminate answer choices, it is essential to develop a systematic approach. Here are a few approaches that can help you become more proficient in this skill:

1. Identify keywords: Read the question carefully and identify any keywords or phrases that stand out. These keywords can help you understand the main idea or concept being tested.

2. Evaluate extremes: Look for answer choices that contain extreme language such as "always," "never," or "none." These choices are often incorrect as they tend to oversimplify complex situations.

3. Pay attention to qualifiers: Notice words like "most," "least," "sometimes," or "usually." These qualifiers can provide clues about the correct answer and help you eliminate choices that do not align with the given information.

4. Use the process of elimination: Start by eliminating the answer choices that are clearly incorrect based on your knowledge or the information provided in the question. Cross them out or mentally discard them to narrow down your options.

5. Review the remaining choices: Once you have eliminated some answer choices, carefully review the remaining options, considering the main idea, context, and any clues provided in the question. This step requires critical thinking and analysis to make an informed decision.

By practicing the skill of eliminating answer choices, you can improve your overall performance on the TEAS exam. Remember, this strategy takes time to develop, so it is crucial to dedicate ample practice to honing this skill. With consistent effort and a systematic approach, you will become more confident in selecting the correct answer, even in challenging scenarios.

In conclusion, mastering the art of eliminating answer choices is a valuable tool for success on the TEAS exam. Aspiring nurses preparing for nursing school should invest time and effort into practicing this skill. By developing a systematic approach, analyzing keywords, evaluating extremes, paying attention to qualifiers, and using the process of elimination, test takers can increase their chances of selecting the correct answer. With consistent practice and dedication, aspiring nurses can confidently approach the TEAS exam and achieve their goals of entering nursing school.

Effective Guessing Strategies

When it comes to the TEAS exam, guessing correctly can make all the difference in your final score. While it is important to thoroughly study and prepare for the exam, sometimes you may encounter questions that leave you stumped. In such situations, having effective guessing strategies can help you increase your chances of selecting the correct answer. Here are some tips to help you improve your guessing skills and boost your performance on the TEAS exam.

1. Process of elimination: One of the most effective guessing strategies is to eliminate the obviously incorrect answers. Read each option carefully and cross out any choices that you know are incorrect. By narrowing down the possibilities, you increase your chances of selecting the correct answer.

2. Context clues: Pay attention to the information given in the question itself. Sometimes, the context can provide valuable clues that help you make an educated guess. Look for keywords or phrases that point towards a specific answer and use them as hints.

3. Educated guesses: If you can eliminate some options but are still unsure of the correct answer, make an educated guess based on your knowledge and understanding of the subject matter. Use your reasoning skills and consider what seems most plausible given the context of the question.

4. Prioritize questions: When taking the TEAS exam, it's important to manage your time effectively. If you encounter a particularly challenging question, don't waste too much time on it. Instead, make an educated guess or mark it for review and move on to the next question. By prioritizing your time, you ensure that you have enough time left for questions that you can answer confidently.

5. Trust your instincts: Sometimes, your initial gut feeling can lead you to the correct answer. If you have narrowed down the options and none of them stands out as the obvious choice, go with your intuition. Often, your subconscious mind can pick up on subtle clues that your conscious mind may miss.

Remember, guessing should be your last resort. It is always better to have a solid understanding of the material and be able to answer questions confidently. However, having effective guessing strategies in your arsenal can help you when you encounter challenging questions on the TEAS exam. Practice these strategies during your TEAS exam practice tests and quizzes to improve your guessing skills and increase your chances of success on the actual exam. Good luck!

Tips for Managing Test Anxiety

Test anxiety is a common experience for many individuals, especially when it comes to important exams such as the TEAS (Test of Essential Academic Skills). For aspiring nurses who are preparing to take the TEAS exam, managing test anxiety is crucial to performing at your best. Here are some helpful tips to help you overcome test anxiety and succeed in your TEAS exam:

1. Prepare and Practice: One of the most effective ways to reduce test anxiety is to be well-prepared. Start studying early and create a study schedule that allows for regular review and practice. By familiarizing yourself with the content and format of the TEAS exam through practice tests and quizzes, you will gain confidence and reduce anxiety.

2. Create a Positive Study Environment: Find a quiet and comfortable place to study where you can focus without distractions. Surround yourself with positive affirmations and motivational quotes to keep your spirits high. Ensure your study area is well-lit and organized, allowing for easy access to study materials.

3. Practice Stress-Relief Techniques: Implement stress-relief techniques such as deep breathing exercises, meditation, or yoga. These techniques can help calm your mind and relax your body, reducing anxiety levels. Take short breaks during study sessions to engage in these activities and recharge your energy.

4. Get Adequate Sleep and Exercise: Prioritize your physical well-being by getting enough sleep and engaging in regular exercise. Sleep deprivation can exacerbate anxiety, while exercise releases endorphins, which help alleviate stress and improve mood.

5. Stay Positive and Manage Negative Thoughts: Replace negative thoughts and self-doubt with positive affirmations. Remind yourself of your strengths and accomplishments. Visualize success and believe in your abilities. Surround yourself with supportive individuals who can help boost your confidence.

6. Time Management: Create a study timetable that allows for breaks and rest. Avoid cramming and distribute your study sessions over a longer period. This will help prevent burnout and reduce anxiety associated with time constraints.

7. Seek Support: Reach out to friends, family, or classmates who are also preparing for the TEAS exam. Discuss your concerns and anxieties with them. Sharing your experiences can provide valuable support and reassurance.

Remember, managing test anxiety is a process. It takes time and practice to find what works best for you. By implementing these tips and strategies, you can reduce test anxiety and perform at your best during the TEAS exam. Stay positive, stay focused, and believe in yourself - success awaits you in your nursing journey!

Congratulations on taking the first step towards your dream of becoming a nurse! As you embark on your journey to nursing school, it is crucial to prepare yourself for the TEAS (Test of Essential Academic Skills) exam. This book will provide you with the essential tools to ace your TEAS exam.

Chapter 8: Conclusion and Next Steps

Assessing Your TEAS Exam Performance

One of the most crucial steps in preparing for the TEAS (Test of Essential Academic Skills) exam is assessing your performance. This subchapter will guide you on how to evaluate your strengths and weaknesses and develop a strategic study plan to excel in your exam.

As an aspiring nurse, it is essential to understand that the TEAS exam plays a significant role in your nursing school application process. This comprehensive assessment evaluates your knowledge in four key areas: Reading, Mathematics, Science, and English and Language Usage. By assessing your performance effectively, you can identify areas where you need to focus more and areas where you are already strong.

To start assessing your TEAS exam performance, it is crucial to take practice tests and quizzes. These practice materials are specifically designed to replicate the actual exam and provide you with an accurate measure of your knowledge and skills. By practicing under exam-like conditions, you can gauge your performance realistically and identify any areas of weakness.

Once you have completed a practice test or quiz, it is essential to thoroughly review your answers. Read through the explanations provided for each question, whether you got it right or wrong. This step will help you understand the reasoning behind the correct answers and identify any gaps in your knowledge. Take note of the topics and question types that consistently challenge you to develop a focused study plan.

After reviewing your answers, gather the data on your performance. Identify your strengths and weaknesses in each of the four TEAS exam sections. Ask yourself: which sections did you excel in? Which sections require more attention? This analysis will be the foundation of your study plan.

With a clear understanding of your strengths and weaknesses, it's time to develop a strategic study plan. Allocate more time to the sections where you struggle the most, while still reinforcing your strengths. Utilize study materials such as textbooks, online resources, and flashcards to enhance your knowledge in the identified areas.

Furthermore, consider seeking additional support. Join study groups or find a tutor who can guide you through the challenging topics. Engaging in discussions with peers and experts will deepen your understanding and provide valuable insights.

Remember, assessing your TEAS exam performance is an ongoing process. Regularly monitor your progress by taking practice tests and quizzes to evaluate your improvement. Adjust your study plan accordingly based on your performance outcomes.

By effectively assessing your TEAS exam performance, you will be better equipped to excel in the exam and increase your chances of getting into nursing school. Stay focused, motivated, and committed to your study plan, and success will be within reach.

Developing a Study Schedule for Continued Preparation

Preparing for the TEAS exam is a crucial step for anyone aspiring to become a nurse. To excel in this exam, it is essential to develop a study schedule that allows for continued learning and practice. This subchapter aims to provide valuable insights and strategies for creating an effective study plan tailored to your needs.

The first step in developing a study schedule is to set clear goals. Determine the date of your TEAS exam and work backward, dividing your study time into manageable chunks. Consider the amount of material you need to cover and allocate sufficient time for each topic. Setting realistic goals will help you stay motivated and focused throughout your preparation.

Next, it is important to identify your strengths and weaknesses. Take practice tests and quizzes to assess your knowledge and identify areas that require further improvement. Once you have identified your weak areas, allocate more time for studying those topics. However, make sure to revise your strong areas as well to maintain a well-rounded understanding of the exam material.

Creating a routine is essential for maintaining discipline and consistency in your study schedule. Determine the most suitable time of the day when you feel most alert and productive. Designate specific time slots for studying each topic, allowing for breaks in between to prevent burnout. Consistency is key, so try to stick to your schedule as much as possible.

To enhance your learning experience, explore various study materials and resources. Consider investing in TEAS exam practice books, online courses, or study guides. These resources offer a comprehensive overview of the exam content and provide sample questions and quizzes to gauge your understanding. Additionally, join study groups or find a study buddy to share knowledge and exchange study tips.

Flexibility is crucial in any study schedule. Be open to making adjustments as you progress through your preparation. If you find that certain topics require more time, be prepared to adjust your schedule accordingly. Remember, the goal is to understand the material thoroughly, so don't rush through it.

In conclusion, developing a study schedule for continued preparation is essential for success in the TEAS exam. By setting clear goals, identifying strengths and weaknesses, creating a routine, exploring study resources, and allowing for flexibility, you can optimize your study efforts and increase your chances of achieving a high score. Remember to stay motivated, maintain discipline, and believe in your abilities. Good luck on your journey to becoming a nurse!

Additional Resources for TEAS Exam Review

As you prepare to embark on your journey to nursing school, it is essential to equip yourself with the right tools and resources to succeed in the TEAS exam. This subchapter aims to provide you with a comprehensive list of additional resources that will enhance your TEAS exam review and help you excel in the test.

1. Online TEAS Exam Practice Tests: Practice makes perfect, and online TEAS exam practice tests are an excellent way to familiarize yourself with the format and content of the exam. These tests simulate the actual exam experience, allowing you to assess your strengths and weaknesses and identify areas that require further study.

2. TEAS Exam Review Books: In addition to "TEAS Exam Essentials: Practice Questions and Quizzes for Aspiring Nurses," various other review books are available in the market. These resources offer in-depth explanations, study tips, and practice questions that cover all sections of the TEAS exam, including Reading, Math, Science, and English.

3. TEAS Exam Review Courses: If you prefer a more structured approach to your TEAS exam review, enrolling in a TEAS exam review course can be highly beneficial. These courses are designed to provide comprehensive coverage of all exam topics, offer expert guidance, and provide additional practice materials to ensure your success.

4. Flashcards: Flashcards are a handy study tool for memorizing key concepts, definitions, and formulas. They are portable and can be taken anywhere, allowing you to review during short breaks or while on the go. Many websites and mobile apps offer pre-made TEAS exam flashcards, or you can create your own based on the areas you find challenging.

5. Study Groups and Forums: Joining a study group or participating in online forums can provide a collaborative learning environment. Engaging with peers who are also preparing for the TEAS exam allows you to exchange ideas, clarify doubts, and gain valuable insights into exam strategies. It can also provide a sense of camaraderie and motivation during the preparation process.

6. Official TEAS Exam Resources: The official TEAS exam website offers a wealth of resources, including study guides, sample questions, and practice exams. These resources are directly aligned with the exam content and provide an accurate representation of what to expect on test day.

Remember, the key to success in the TEAS exam lies in consistent and focused preparation. Utilizing these additional resources along with this book will help you build confidence, improve your performance, and increase your chances of achieving your goal of becoming a nurse.

Appendix: TEAS Exam Resources and References

In this appendix, you will find a comprehensive list of TEAS exam resources and references to help you prepare for your journey into nursing school. Aspiring nurses face the challenge of passing the TEAS exam, a crucial step in gaining admission to nursing programs. To assist you in your preparation, we have compiled a range of practice tests and quizzes to ensure you are well-prepared for exam day.

1. TEAS Exam Practice Tests:
To excel in the TEAS exam, it is essential to practice with actual exam-like questions. This section includes a collection of practice tests that mirror the structure and content of the TEAS exam. Each test covers all four major areas: Reading, Mathematics, Science, and English Language Usage. By regularly taking these practice tests, you will be able to assess your progress and identify areas requiring additional focus.

2. TEAS Exam Quizzes:
Quizzes are an excellent way to reinforce your understanding of specific concepts. We have designed a series of TEAS exam quizzes that focus on individual topics within the four major areas. These quizzes will help you gauge your comprehension level and identify areas that need further attention. Regular practice with these quizzes will boost your confidence and ensure you are well-prepared for the exam.

3. Recommended Study Guides:
To supplement your practice tests and quizzes, we have compiled a list of highly recommended study guides specifically tailored for the TEAS exam. These guides provide detailed explanations of key concepts, sample questions, and tips to improve your test-taking strategies. Make sure to consult these resources to enhance your overall preparation and increase your chances of success.

4. Online Resources:
The internet is a treasure trove of valuable resources for TEAS exam preparation. We have curated a list of reputable websites, online forums, and study communities where you can find additional practice questions, study materials, and peer support. These online resources can provide a collaborative learning environment and offer insights from individuals who have successfully passed the TEAS exam.

Remember, success in the TEAS exam requires consistent practice, dedication, and a comprehensive understanding of the exam content. Utilize the resources and references provided in this appendix to enhance your preparation and increase your chances of achieving your dream of becoming a nurse. Good luck on your TEAS exam journey!

Note: It is important to keep in mind that the availability and relevance of specific resources and references may change over time. Be sure to check for updated editions or newer resources to ensure you have the most current and effective tools for your TEAS exam preparation.

Made in the USA
Columbia, SC
18 January 2025